I0479114

THE

GOLDEN

LOVE:

ETERNAL BOND OF PURE AFFECTION, A

TIMELESS ROMANCE OF SPLENDOR.

BY:

ROLANDO D. PIERSON

TABLE OF CONTENT

INTRODUCTION

In a world that often seems cold and brutal, love has the potential to alter lives and inspire greatness. It may bring people together, heal old wounds, and light the darkest recesses of the human heart. So what happens when love becomes an obsession? When it absorbs us fully, blinding us to everything else? And what happens when that love is endangered by the same forces that brought it to life?

Love, the most powerful and incomprehensible force in the universe. It has the capacity to convert a drab and gloomy existence into one full of pleasure and excitement. It is the driving force behind every great narrative, every inspirational tale, and every spectacular experience. Love is not simply a sensation, it's an emotion that envelops our existence and fills us with a sense of fullness. It is a force that cannot be seen or touched, but its influence is felt far and wide. Love has the capacity to heal the wounded, repair the broken, and bring people together from all walks of life. It is a global language that transcends all frontiers and brings us closer to one another. Love is the reason why we exist, it's the foundation around which our lives are constructed. It is a gift that we should preserve, cultivate, and defend because it is the one thing that actually makes life worth living.

No human being can do away with love since love has numerous forms and arrives in varied dimensions. There are a number of definitions of love from a range of individuals but what truly is Golden Love?

Individuals erroneously fall in love and believe they have the golden love to succeed in their love journey. Weeks and months pass by and what they hypothesized about their love was only an illusion.

Keep following this book to read through the pages to grasp what the real love that you are seeking truly implies, the idea of love, and the characters to create your love an everlasting one.

CHAPTER ONE

The Definition of Love

Love is one of the most intense and complicated human emotions. It is an idea that has been examined, written about, and investigated by poets, philosophers, psychologists, and neuroscientists for centuries. But despite all of our efforts to describe and explain love, it remains a mystery that resists simple explanation.

At its most fundamental level, love is a sense of affection or devotion towards someone or something. It might be romantic or platonic, aimed towards a person, animal, location, or even a concept. Love is typically connected with pleasant feelings such as pleasure, happiness, and satisfaction, but it may also be accompanied by negative emotions such as jealousy, rage, and despair.

One of the most intriguing things about love is how it can take on so many various shapes and meanings depending on the environment and society in which it is expressed. For example, in Western countries, romantic love is generally depicted as the ultimate objective of a relationship, yet in other cultures, such as those in parts of Asia, love may be considered more as a responsibility or obligation towards family or community.

In addition to cultural variances, love may also vary based on individual experience and perspective. Some individuals would characterize love as a sense of passion and intensity, while others might perceive it as a deep and persistent relationship that grows through time. For some, love is a source of comfort and stability, while for others, it is a source of struggle and progress.

Despite these disparities, there are certain constants in how love is experienced and understood across cultures and people. Love frequently encompasses sentiments of warmth, compassion, and care for another person or object. Passion may motivate us to behave selflessly and to make sacrifices for the well-being of the people we love. Love may also be a source of strength and endurance during tough times, allowing us to endure trials and conquer hurdles.

Nevertheless, love is not always a beneficial force. It may be accompanied by negative feelings such as jealousy, possessiveness, and even violence in severe circumstances. Love may also lead to disappointment and heartache when our expectations are not realized, or when relationships terminate.

Several researchers have sought to classify distinct forms of love based on their traits and characteristics. For example, the ancient Greeks classified four distinct sorts of love: eros, philia, agape, and storge. Eros refers to passionate or romantic love, whereas philia is a deep and lasting friendship love. Agape is selfless and unconditional love, whereas storge is a family or loving love.

Several theories of love emphasize the function of attachment and bonding in romantic relationships. According to attachment theory, our early experiences with caregivers impact our potential to develop healthy bonds with love partners later in life. These attachments might be secure, apprehensive, or avoidant, and can impact our patterns of behavior and emotional reactions in relationships.

Ultimately, love is a complicated and multidimensional feeling that resists simple explanation. It may take on many various shapes and meanings depending on the environment and culture in which it is presented. Love may be a source of pleasure and connection, but it can also be a cause of heartache and disappointment. Despite its complications, love remains one of the most powerful and transformational forces in human experience, affecting our relationships, our sense of ourselves, and our perception of the world around us.

Triangle Theory of Love

The triangular theory of love is a hypothesis that describes how love develops and how it may be assessed. The idea was initially proposed by Robert Sternberg in 1986, and it has since been extensively explored and utilized in several domains, including psychology, sociology, and anthropology. The triangle theory of love posits that love is made up of three components, namely closeness, passion, and commitment, which interact in various ways to generate distinct forms of love.

The first component of the triangle theory of love is intimacy, which refers to the emotional relationship between two persons. This component comprises emotions of warmth, intimacy, and trust, and it is generally connected with love partnerships. Intimacy is generally defined as the exchange of personal information, emotional support, and physical love. This component is crucial for building a deep and lasting relationship with someone, and it frequently develops slowly over time.

The second component of the triangle theory of love is passion, which refers to the physical and sexual attraction between two persons. This component is generally characterized by extreme feelings, such as want, passion, and excitement. Passionate love is frequently characterized by a strong physical and sexual desire, and it often incorporates emotions of infatuation and obsession. This component is often connected with the early phases of a romantic relationship, and it might wane over time or evolve into a more durable kind of love.

The third component of the triangle theory of love is commitment, which refers to the choice to sustain a long-term connection with someone. This component comprises the commitment to work through challenges and conflicts, to value the relationship above individual wants and goals, and to make sacrifices for the other person. Commitment is frequently viewed as the cornerstone of an enduring and meaningful relationship, and it is defined by a feeling of duty, devotion, and loyalty.

According to the triangle theory of love, various varieties of love may be generated by mixing these three components in different ways. For example, Sternberg postulated seven distinct varieties of love based on the combinations of closeness, passion, and commitment. These kinds include:

1. Liking: This sort of love is characterized by a strong feeling of closeness but little or no passion or commitment. It is typically found in intimate friendships and platonic partnerships.

2. Infatuation: This sort of love is characterized by tremendous desire but little or no closeness or commitment. It is commonly connected with the early phases of a love relationship and may disappear fast.

3. Empty love: This sort of love is defined by dedication but little or no closeness or passion. It is

typically observed in arranged marriages or long-term partnerships that have lost their spark.

4. Romantic love: This sort of love is characterized by a high feeling of closeness and passion but little or no commitment. It is typically found in casual partnerships or short-term romances.

5. Companionate love: This sort of love is characterized by a strong feeling of closeness and commitment but little or no passion. It is commonly found in long-term partnerships, like marriages or close friendships.

6. Fatuous love: This sort of love is characterized by tremendous passion and dedication but little or no closeness. It is typically found in relationships that are based on infatuation or physical desire.

7. Consummate love: This sort of love is characterized by a great feeling of closeness, desire, and commitment. It is often seen as the ideal form of love and is the goal of most romantic relationships.

The triangle theory of love has various implications for our understanding of love and relationships. For example, it indicates that love is not a simple and uncomplicated feeling but a complex and multifaceted construct that comprises many components. It also argues that multiple varieties of love may be generated based on the combinations of these components and that certain types of love are more desired and durable than others. Moreover, the triangle theory of love says that love is not static but dynamic and may vary over time when the components of intimacy, passion, and commitment alter in a relationship.

The triangle theory of love also has practical implications in the world of therapy and counseling. For example, therapists might utilize the theory to assist couples to understand the many components of love and how they interact with one another. By understanding which components are missing in a relationship, therapists may help couples work towards building a more balanced and satisfied love connection. The idea may also assist people to understand their love patterns and preferences, which can help them make better-informed judgments regarding their relationships.

One of the drawbacks of the triangle theory of love is that it may not be universally relevant across cultures. The hypothesis was formed based on research on Western, educated, industrialized, affluent, and democratic (WEIRD) cultures, which may not reflect the range of human experiences and values. Other cultures may put greater emphasis on certain components of love, such as responsibility, respect, or spirituality, which are not included in the triangle theory of love. Also, certain cultures may perceive the various varieties of love differently, such as perceiving companionate love as the ideal form of love rather than consummate love.

The triangle theory of love offers a valuable framework for understanding how love develops and how it may be quantified. The theory proposes that love is made up of three components, namely intimacy, passion, and commitment, which combine in different ways to form different types of love. The theory has practical applications in the field of therapy and counseling and can help individuals and couples understand their love patterns and preferences. Nevertheless, the hypothesis may not be universally relevant across cultures, and greater study is required to understand the cultural and environmental aspects that impact the formation and expression of love.

The Many Facets of Love.

Love is one of the most complicated feelings that people experience. It has many various elements, and each individual feels it in their manner. Love may be romantic, platonic, family, or even spiritual. It may be conveyed in numerous ways, such as via acts of service, physical contact, quality time, and words of affirmation. In the next pages, we will study the different dimensions of love and how they impact our interactions with others.

1. Romantic Love

Romantic love is a unique and strong sort of love that is frequently connected with deep emotions, passion, and physical attraction between two individuals. It is defined by a profound connection and dedication to another person, typically culminating in long-term relationships, marriage, or even lifetime partnerships. One of the fundamental elements of romantic love is the powerful sensations of infatuation and passion that typically accompany it. Individuals in romantic love typically experience a sensation of elation, excitement, and delight while they are with their spouse. They may feel a surge of adrenaline, heightened perceptions, and tremendous physical attraction, which may lead to sexual desire and close physical contact.

In addition to physical attraction, romantic love is also defined by emotional connection and closeness. Individuals in romantic love frequently have a close emotional connection with their spouse, sharing their ideas, emotions, and aspirations. They may experience a feeling of security and ease in their partner's presence, which may give a solid foundation for the relationship to grow and flourish. Romantic love may also be defined by a feeling of exclusivity and commitment. Individuals in love partnerships generally prioritize their partner above others, spending time and energy into creating and sustaining the connection. They may feel a feeling of responsibility for their partner's happiness and well-being and may make sacrifices to support their partner's ambitions and desires. But, passionate love is not always simple or without its problems. Partnerships may be difficult and involve work, patience, and compromise to flourish. Individuals in love relationships may suffer tension, jealousy, and even grief when things don't go as expected. Despite the hurdles, many individuals consider romantic love to be one of the most gratifying and significant experiences in life. It may bring a feeling of purpose, friendship, and satisfaction, and can serve as a source of strength and support through tough times. Eventually, romantic love may be a strong force that influences our lives and offers pleasure and satisfaction to those who experience it.

2. Platonic Love

Platonic love is a sort of love that stresses the emotional and spiritual connection between persons rather than physical desire. It is named after the ancient Greek philosopher, Plato, who felt that love was an intellectual and spiritual relationship that transcended physical attraction.

Unlike other types of love, such as romantic or sexual love, platonic love is non-sexual. It includes a profound emotional relationship between two persons who share similar interests, beliefs, and values. This form of love is generally represented as a love between friends when the connection is founded on mutual respect, appreciation, and a desire to see the other person prosper. One of the major elements of platonic love is the lack of sexual desire. Although sexual desire may be a feature of a romantic relationship, platonic love doesn't have to exist. In reality, the lack of sexual desire enables a stronger emotional connection to emerge between two persons. Platonic love is frequently considered a purer kind of love since it is not driven by bodily wants. Platonic love may be a significant influence on people's lives. It may give a feeling of emotional support, camaraderie, and understanding that is not always accessible in other relationships. Platonic love may also be transforming, driving people to become better versions of themselves and supporting personal development. Plato felt that platonic love was the finest type of love since it entailed a strong connection between two persons' souls. He maintained that physical attraction was transient and could not compare to the lifelong emotional tie that might be developed via platonic love. Platonic love was considered a method of obtaining personal enlightenment and a connection to the divine. In modern society, platonic love is commonly represented in popular cultures, such as movies and television series, as a sort of love between friends. It is a sort of love that is typically admired for its purity and the emotional relationship it generates between persons. This is a sort of love that is defined by a strong emotional and spiritual connection between persons. It highlights the need for reciprocal respect, appreciation, and a desire to see the other person develop. Platonic love is non-sexual, which allows for a stronger emotional attachment to form between persons. It is a powerful force in people's lives, providing emotional support, companionship, and understanding that is not always possible in other relationships. Plato felt that platonic love was the greatest type of love since it entailed a strong connection between two persons' souls and a method of gaining personal enlightenment.

3. Familial Love

Familial love, also known as familial affection or family love, is a sort of love that is often experienced among family members. It is a link that is developed via blood ties, shared experiences, and a profound feeling of belonging. Familial love is defined by sentiments of loyalty, protectiveness, and unconditional support. One of the most distinguishing aspects of family love is its capacity to persist throughout time. Family members may not always get along or agree on everything, yet the tie between them stays strong. This is because family love is not based on exterior characteristics such as beauty or fortune, but on a shared history and a feeling of belonging.

Familial love may take various forms. It might be the love between parents and children, between siblings, or between extended family members such as grandparents, aunts, and uncles. In each situation, the link is established on a basis of trust, understanding, and mutual respect. One of the most significant qualities of family love is its capacity to assist through tough times. When a family member is going through a terrible phase, whether it be a health crisis, financial hardship, or emotional strain, other family members frequently gather around them to give comfort, counsel, and practical aid. This support network may be a source of tremendous comfort and strength, allowing family members to face obstacles that would otherwise seem insurmountable.

Familial love may also be a source of pleasure and happiness. Family members typically share a great feeling of pride in one another's successes, whether it be a child's scholastic success, a sibling's work achievements, or a grandparent's life achievements. This shared feeling of pride may establish a strong relationship between family members, and assist to form a pleasant, supportive family dynamic.

Familial love is a strong force that can alter our lives in significant ways. It is a relationship that is founded on a foundation of shared experiences, trust, and mutual respect, and it offers us a feeling of belonging, support, and unconditional love that is difficult to find anywhere else. Whether we are parents, children, siblings, or extended family members, familial love is a sort of love that enriches our lives and allows us to negotiate the ups and downs of life with grace and fortitude.

4. Spiritual Love

Spiritual love may also be experienced in connections with other people. When two individuals have a strong feeling of spiritual connection, they might experience a degree of closeness and understanding that goes beyond the physical and emotional. This sort of connection is frequently characterized by a feeling of unconditional love and acceptance, where each person feels seen, heard, and understood in a manner that is profoundly transforming.

Spiritual love is a sort of love that is defined by a profound connection that goes beyond the physical and emotional. It may be experienced via a connection with nature, meditation or prayer, or interactions with other people. This sort of love is frequently connected with a feeling of enlightenment or awakening and maybe a transformational experience for those who seek it out.

5. Self-Love

Self-love is the love that one has for oneself. It is frequently defined by a feeling of acceptance, respect, and concern for one's well-being. This form of love is necessary for a healthy and successful existence, as it enables people to prioritize their wants and ideals.

Self-love may be expressed in numerous ways, such as via self-care activities, creating healthy boundaries, or practicing self-compassion. It is typically a source of inner strength and resilience, helping people to face life's adversities with more ease and grace.

Self-love is a sort of love that entails a person having favorable respect and acceptance towards oneself. It comprises a spectrum of acts and attitudes that enhance one's well-being, progress, and self-acceptance. Self-love is frequently referred to as the cornerstone of a healthy and happy existence. It is the practice of treating oneself with the same compassion, kindness and care that one would show to a valued friend or family member.

Self-love is embracing oneself for who one is, warts and all. It entails identifying and appreciating one's talents and limitations and taking efforts toward personal growth and development. It also involves being nice to oneself and avoiding self-criticism and negative self-talk. By treating themselves with love and compassion, people are better equipped to take care of themselves and traverse life's problems with more ease.

Self-love is not the same as self-absorption or narcissism. Rather, it is a healthy and balanced attitude to self-care that helps people to have full lives and develop great connections with others.

When people practice self-love, they are more suited to build meaningful connections with others, as they can approach relationships from a position of strength, rather than neediness or insecurity.

Self-love may take various forms, such as participating in activities that offer pleasure and satisfaction, creating boundaries, prioritizing one's needs, and engaging in self-care practices like exercise, meditation, and good nutrition. It may also entail fostering self-awareness, practicing appreciation, and having a happy mentality.

Although self-love is vital for everyone, it is especially critical for persons who have undergone trauma or tough life situations. By establishing a feeling of self-love and self-acceptance, people are better equipped to recover from previous hurts and move on with more resilience.

In conclusion, self-love is a fundamental part of our total well-being and pleasure. It entails treating oneself with love, compassion, and respect, and creating a healthy connection with oneself. By practicing self-love, people are better able to overcome life's problems, develop meaningful relationships, and live fulfilled lives.

Complexities of Human Emotions

Human beings are complicated creatures with a huge spectrum of emotions that govern their conduct and impact their actions. Understanding the complexity of human emotion is vital for persons in numerous disciplines, including psychology, social work, education, and healthcare, to give the best care and support to their clients. It is a complicated area of research that encompasses a profound knowledge of the neurological, physiological, and psychological elements of emotion.

Emotions are complex, subjective experiences that comprise a variety of physiological, cognitive, and behavioral reactions. They are generally triggered by external stimuli, including events, people, and circumstances. Emotions may be good, such as joy, love, and enthusiasm, or negative, such as wrath, fear, and despair. They may also be complicated and mixed, such as ambivalence and guilt. Understanding the complexity of human emotion demands an in-depth study of its numerous aspects.

The physiological component of emotion is one of the most essential characteristics of human emotions. Emotions are typically accompanied by physiological changes, such as increased heart rate, perspiration, and changes in facial expression. These physiological reactions are governed by the autonomic nerve system, which is responsible for regulating our physical processes. The autonomic nervous system is split into two branches: the sympathetic and the parasympathetic branches. The sympathetic branch is responsible for generating the body's fight or flight response, while the parasympathetic branch is responsible for bringing the body to a state of relaxation. The connection between these two branches plays a critical role in the physiological component of emotions.

The cognitive component of emotion is another key part of understanding the complexity of human emotion. It includes the mental processes that occur when we feel emotions. This dimension encompasses how we understand, assess, and react to emotions. For example, our perception of a circumstance might impact our emotional reaction to it. If we see a situation as dangerous, we may sense dread or anxiety, whereas experiencing it as an opportunity may stimulate excitement or pleasure. Our ideas, values, and prior experiences also impact our cognitive reactions to emotions.

The behavioral component of emotion is equally significant in comprehending the intricacies of human emotion. It includes the outer displays of our emotions, such as our facial expressions, body language, and vocal communication. Our conduct may impact the emotions of others, and in turn, our emotions can influence the behavior of others. For example, a grin may be infectious and can generate a pleasant emotional milieu, whereas an angry outburst might induce dread or worry in others.

Another challenge in comprehending human emotions is the subjective character of emotions. Emotions are subjective sensations that are unique to each person. Individuals may experience the same circumstance yet have distinct emotional reactions.

For example, one individual may find a rollercoaster ride thrilling, while another may find it horrifying. The subjective character of emotions makes it tough to quantify and compare emotions effectively.

Additionally, emotions may be altered by cultural and societal variables. Many cultures and communities have specific emotional norms and expectations that impact how people perceive and express emotions. For example, in certain cultures, expressing anger or grief may be deemed unacceptable, while in others, it may be welcomed as a form of emotional expression.

In conclusion, grasping the intricacies of human emotion needs a profound comprehension of its different components, including the physiological, cognitive, and behavioral elements. Emotions are subjective sensations that are unique to each person, making it tough to quantify and compare emotions correctly. Moreover, cultural and societal influences might impact how people perceive and express emotions. Good knowledge of human emotion is needed in several professions, including psychology, social work, education, and healthcare, to give the best care and assistance to clients.

Love: An Intensely Intimate and Subjective Feeling.

Love is a deeply intimate and subjective sensation that is impossible to explain or measure. It may take numerous forms and can be perceived in different ways by different individuals. The emotion of love is typically characterized as a warm and fuzzy sense that may leave us feeling happy and pleased. But, the intricacy of love also means that it may be difficult to grasp, and it can be tricky to manage the intricacies of human relationships.

One of the reasons why love is such a personal and subjective feeling is because it is strongly related to our particular experiences and viewpoints. For example, the way we see love may be impacted by our upbringing, cultural background, and personal beliefs. Also, our prior experiences of love or lack thereof might mold our notions of what love is and what it should feel like.

The intensity of love may also vary widely from person to person, and even within the same individual over time. For others, love is a passionate and all-consuming sensation that may take over their whole existence. For others, love may be a quieter and more subtle feeling that is communicated via tiny gestures and acts of kindness.

One of the most essential features of love is that it is generally tied to a desire for connection and closeness with another person. Human beings are social animals, and the desire for companionship and emotional support is profoundly embedded in our nature. Love creates a feeling of belonging and acceptance that is crucial to our well-being.

But, the need for love and connection may also leave us susceptible to emotional anguish and heartache. When we engage our emotions in another person, we put ourselves up to the prospect of rejection, disappointment, and loss. The dread of these undesirable effects may often cause us to shun love completely, or to become guarded and careful in our relationships.

Despite the hazards involved, love remains one of the most sought-after sensations in human existence. Passion is a strong force that may motivate us to be our best selves and to seek greater knowledge of ourselves and others. Love may also be a source of healing and development, allowing us to overcome previous traumas and develop a better sense of compassion and empathy.

It is also worth mentioning that love is not necessarily restricted to romantic partnerships. We may feel love for our friends, family members, and even pets. The link between a father and child, for example, is typically regarded as one of the most intense manifestations of love that exists. This larger definition of love underscores the fact that it is a universal and vital part of human existence.

Another feature that makes love such a personal and subjective feeling is that it may emerge in various ways at different phases of our life. The love we feel as children for our parents or siblings may be completely different from the romantic love we experience as adults. Similarly, the love we feel for a long-term spouse may vary and alter over time, as we negotiate the ups and downs of life together.

Some theories of love concentrate more on the numerous varieties of love that exist. The ancient Greeks, for example, distinguished numerous different varieties of love, including eros (romantic or sexual love), philia (friendship or loving love), and agape (unconditional or selfless love) (unconditional or altruistic love). These numerous models and theories of love underline the fact that it is a multidimensional and complicated feeling that is impossible to explain separately.

Love is a deeply personal and subjective feeling that may take numerous shapes and be experienced in different ways by different individuals. It is strongly related to our particular experiences and viewpoints, therefore it may be difficult to describe or measure.

The intensity of love may vary widely from person to person, and it can emerge in various ways at different phases of our life. Love is also intimately tied to a need for connection and closeness with another person, and it may be a source of healing and development.

Despite the hurdles and dangers associated with seeking love, it remains one of the deepest and most significant experiences that we can have as human beings. Love can inspire us, offer us pleasure, and assist us to become better versions of ourselves. It is a crucial component of our emotional and social life, and it gives us a feeling of purpose and belonging that is difficult to obtain elsewhere.

One of the most essential things to know about love is that it is not a static or set feeling. Instead, it is a dynamic and growing experience that may vary over time as we manage the intricacies of human interactions. By being open and receptive to the many various forms that love may take, we can improve our relationships with others and find more joy and purpose in our lives.

In conclusion, love is a deeply personal and subjective sensation that is impossible to explain or measure. It may take numerous forms and be experienced in different ways by different individuals. The intensity of love may vary widely from person to person, and it can emerge in various ways at different phases of our life. Despite the hurdles and dangers associated with seeking love, it remains one of the deepest and most significant experiences that we can have as human beings. By accepting the many various forms that love may take, we can discover more connection, pleasure, and satisfaction in our lives.

The Science of Love.

Although love is typically thought of as a purely emotional experience, it also has significant ties to the brain and the body, with a vast variety of physiological and chemical processes involved in the feeling of falling in love.

One of the most essential components in the science of love is the impact of neurotransmitters such as dopamine, oxytocin, and serotonin. Dopamine, for example, is commonly related to emotions of pleasure and reward and is produced at significant levels when we encounter something good or interesting. This includes romantic experiences, such as spending time with a loved one or indulging in intimate physical contact. Similarly, oxytocin is commonly nicknamed the "love hormone" since it is produced at moments of social bonding and physical touch, such as embracing or kissing.

Serotonin is another neurotransmitter that has a function in the sensation of love. It is important in regulating mood and anxiety, and when levels of serotonin are low, people may suffer symptoms of sadness or anxiety. This may influence the experience of falling in love, since people who are feeling nervous or sad may find it difficult to connect with others and enjoy the sensations of pleasure that are frequently linked with falling in love.

In addition to neurotransmitters, the brain plays a crucial part in the sensation of love. The prefrontal cortex, for example, is the portion of the brain that is responsible for decision-making, judgment, and planning. It is also involved in the sensation of love, as it allows us to evaluate possible mates and make judgments about who we want to pursue romantic relationships with.

Other regions of the brain that are involved in the sensation of love include the amygdala, which is responsible for processing emotions, and the hippocampus, which is involved in memory formation. These regions of the brain work together to generate a complex and nuanced experience of falling in love, with emotions and memories merging to make a deep and meaningful relationship with a romantic partner.

The science of love also covers the study of attachment types and how they affect our relationships. Attachment styles relate to how people create and sustain strong connections with others, and are typically impacted by early experiences with caregivers. There are four basic attachment styles: secure, anxious-preoccupied, dismissive-avoidant, and fearful-avoidant.

People with a stable attachment type tend to be comfortable with intimacy and can build deep, healthy connections with others. Individuals with an anxious-preoccupied attachment style, on the other hand, may suffer from feelings of insecurity and may be more prone to cling to their relationships. Dismissive-avoidant persons may be reluctant to create personal connections or may avoid emotional intimacy completely, whereas fearful-avoidant individuals may struggle with both closeness and independence.

Understanding attachment types may be beneficial in navigating romantic relationships, as it can assist people to see trends in their conduct and the behavior of their partners. By understanding their attachment type and striving to create healthy behaviors and communication skills, people may enhance the quality of their relationships and build deeper, more meaningful connections with their partners.

Lastly, the science of love also encompasses the study of cultural and societal aspects that shape our experiences of love and relationships. Various cultures may put varying priorities on romantic relationships, for example, with some stressing emotional closeness and others preferring practical concerns such as financial stability or familial connections.

Societal elements such as gender and sexuality also play a part in the feeling of love, with cultural conventions and expectations frequently impacting how people create and sustain romantic relationships. Knowing these cultural and societal elements may allow people to better negotiate the complexity of love relationships and establish deeper, more rewarding bonds with their partners.

In conclusion, the science of love is a complicated and multi-faceted discipline that involves a broad spectrum of physiological, psychological, and social aspects. From the production of neurotransmitters such as dopamine and oxytocin to the functioning of various areas of the brain, the sensation of falling in love is a highly subtle and sophisticated process.

Attachment types also have a key impact on how people create and sustain intimate relationships, and knowing these patterns may be beneficial in creating healthy, rewarding interactions with others.

Lastly, cultural and social variables have a big effect on our experiences of love and relationships, with societal norms and expectations impacting the way we see and approach romantic partnerships.

Ultimately, the science of love is a fascinating and difficult area, with researchers continuing to unearth new insights and understandings about the nature of this strong emotion. By investigating the many diverse aspects that contribute to our experiences of love, we may increase our awareness of ourselves and our relationships, and establish better and more rewarding connections with those around us.

CHAPTER TWO

What is Golden Love?

Golden love is a word used to represent a form of love that is lasting, pure, and steadfast. It is a love that endures the test of time and is marked by great passion, respect, and commitment. Golden love is frequently linked with mature relationships when couples have gone through struggles and hardships together, yet have come out stronger and more in love than ever before.

The phrase "golden" is commonly used to describe anything expensive, uncommon, and precious. Golden love is no exception, as it depicts a form of love that is difficult to obtain but is worth cherishing and developing. It is a love that is not based on superficial attributes, but on a profound connection that transcends physical appeal and financial goods.

Golden love is distinguished by a variety of features that make it stand out from other varieties of love. One of these qualities is loyalty. Couples who share golden love are dedicated to one another and are prepared to go through thick and thin together. They are each other's support system, and are always there for each other, no matter what.

Another attribute that identifies golden love is selflessness. Lovers that share this form of love are prepared to set their wants aside for the benefit of their partner's pleasure. They are ready to make sacrifices and concessions and are continuously seeking ways to demonstrate their love and gratitude.

Golden love is also defined by honesty and transparency. Partners that share this form of love are honest with each other and are open to discussing their views, emotions, and experiences. They speak freely and honestly and are always eager to listen and comprehend each other's opinions.

In addition to these features, golden love is also defined by a strong feeling of respect and appreciation. Partners that share this form of love have great regard for one other's qualities and are eager to assist each other in their goals and objectives. They are each other's greatest admirers and are continuously seeking ways to raise each other and help one another flourish.

Golden love is not only about being happy and satisfied with one another, but it is also about developing and expanding together. Partners that share this form of love are always working on themselves and their relationship, and are always seeking ways to develop and deepen their connection.

In a world where love may sometimes be transitory and shallow, golden love stands out as a beacon of hope and inspiration. It is a love that is lasting and pure and is marked by profound passion, respect, and dedication. Couples who share golden love have discovered something genuinely unique and precious, and are devoted to cherishing and cultivating it for the rest of their lives.

In conclusion, golden love is a sort of love that is defined by loyalty, selflessness, honesty, openness, respect, and appreciation. It is a love that is lasting and genuine and is worth cherishing and cultivating. Couples that share this form of love have discovered something genuinely unique and precious, and are devoted to developing and changing together.

Golden love is a light of hope and inspiration in a world where love can sometimes be transient and shallow, and is something that we should all aim to accomplish in our relationships.

Golden Love Qualities.

Golden Love is a word used to characterize a deep, profound, and long-lasting love connection. It is the sort of love that is uncommon, valuable, and valued by those who experience it. This sort of love is distinguished by particular traits that separate it from other types of love. Here are (10) qualities of Golden Love.

1. Mutual respect

One of the most significant features of Golden Love is mutual respect. This signifies that both spouses have a profound regard for each other's values, views, and viewpoints. They listen to each other with an open mind and without judgment. They are sensitive to one another's emotions and treat each other with respect and compassion.

2. Trust

Trust is another fundamental element of Golden Love. Couples that share Golden Love have a deep feeling of trust in each other. They are sure that their spouse is loyal and dedicated to the relationship. They are also able to confide in one another and reveal their innermost concerns and anxieties.

3. Communication

Excellent communication is key in Golden Love. Lovers that share this sort of love can express themselves freely and honestly. People communicate their thoughts and worries without fear of criticism or rejection. They also listen attentively to each other and attempt to comprehend one another's opinions.

4. Empathy

Empathy is the ability to understand and share the feelings of another person. In Golden Love, lovers feel compassionate towards one another. They can put themselves in their partner's shoes and view things from their perspective. They are attentive to their partner's needs and emotions and make an effort to be helpful and empathetic.

5. Emotional closeness

Emotional closeness is an integral aspect of Golden Love. Couples that share this sort of love are intimately linked on an emotional level. They can disclose their deepest ideas, emotions, and aspirations to one another without fear of criticism. They also feel safe being open with one another and disclosing their innermost worries and concerns.

6. Common beliefs and aims

Couples that share Golden Love have a common vision for their future. They share comparable beliefs and objectives and work together to attain them. They are also able to compromise and make compromises for one other's pleasure and well-being.

7. Physical intimacy

Physical closeness is a crucial part of Golden Love. Couples that share this sort of love have a deep bodily connection with each other. They can show their love via physical contact and tenderness. They also make an effort to emphasize physical connection in their relationship.

8. Forgiveness

Forgiveness is another fundamental feature of Golden Love. Couples who share this sort of love can forgive each other for their faults and inadequacies. They understand that no one is perfect, and they are willing to work through their issues and conflicts with each other.

9. Patience

Patience is a characteristic that is necessary for Golden Love. Couples that share this sort of love are patient with one another. They recognize that love takes time and work to grow and flourish. They are also tolerant of each other's faults and defects, and they attempt to work through their troubles and disagreements with each other.

10. Gratitude

Couples that share Golden Love are thankful for each other. They appreciate the worth and significance of their connection and make an effort to show their thanks to each other. They are thankful for the love, support, and companionship that they share.

These characteristics are essential for building and maintaining a deep, meaningful, and long-lasting romantic relationship. Couples who share Golden Love can navigate the ups and downs of life together and build a strong foundation for their future. Although Golden Love may not be simple to discover or keep, it is worth fighting for.

It is vital to realize that obtaining Golden Love is not something that occurs immediately. It involves effort, patience, and a willingness to work through hurdles and barriers. It is also crucial to note that every relationship is unique and that partners may have their own set of features that characterize their love.

Yet, by adding these 10 traits to your relationship, you may develop a firm basis for long-lasting and meaningful love. Remember to always talk freely and honestly with your spouse, be sensitive and understanding, and prioritize your relationship. With these attributes in mind, you may strive towards developing a Golden Love that will provide you pleasure and joy for years to come.

In addition to these 10 characteristics, it is important to remember that maintaining a healthy relationship also involves other factors such as respect for boundaries, active listening, compromise, and self-reflection. Couples should also focus on their individual development and well-being since a healthy and happy person leads to a good and happy partnership.

In conclusion, Golden Love is a unique and valuable sort of love defined by mutual respect, trust, efficient communication, empathy, emotional intimacy, shared values and objectives, physical closeness, forgiveness, patience, and thankfulness. By combining these traits into your relationship and emphasizing your development and well-being, you may establish a solid foundation for long-lasting and meaningful love.

The Power of Golden Love.

The power of love is one of the most tremendous forces in the world, capable of motivating us to accomplish great things, bringing us together in harmony, and healing even the darkest wounds. Yet there is one form of love that rises above all others, a love that is pure, unselfish, and unconditional. This is the power of the Golden Love.

Golden Love is a word used to express a profound love that surpasses the boundaries of our physical existence. It is a love that comes from the very center of our being, and it is the source of all genuine pleasure and joy. This form of love is not founded on external events or situations, but rather on an inner state of being. It is the sort of love that helps us to connect with people on a deeper level and to perceive the divine spark inside every one of us.

The power of Golden Love may be witnessed in many different realms of life. For example, it is the force that permits a woman to give birth to her kid, and it is the love that leads a father to sacrifice all for the well-being of their child. It is the love that pushes a volunteer to spend their time helping people in need, and it is the love that drives a teacher to encourage their pupils to attain their greatest potential.

Golden Love also can heal. When we are harmed, whether physically or emotionally, it is frequently the love and support of people around us that enables us to recover. This is because Golden Love has the potential to penetrate even the deepest scars and to bring about a feeling of serenity and completeness that cannot be found anywhere else.

Maybe the most significant quality of Golden Love is that it is unconditional. It does not rely on whether the object of our affection is flawless or imperfect, gorgeous or ugly, successful or unsuccessful. It just exists, without judgment or expectation. This implies that when we can tap into the power of Golden Love, we may love ourselves and others unconditionally, and we can achieve a feeling of inner peace and pleasure that is not reliant on external circumstances.

But, tapping into the power of Golden Love is not always simple. We are frequently conditioned by our upbringing and by society to think that love is something that must be earned or that is conditional. We may also have our inner scars and worries that hinder us from completely giving ourselves up to this form of love. Yet with practice and a willingness to let go of our prejudices and concerns, we may begin to access the power of Golden Love inside us.

One approach to harnessing the power of Golden Love is via meditation or other spiritual activities. By quieting the mind and concentrating on the inner state of being, we may begin to connect with the love that lives within us and build a feeling of inner peace and pleasure.

Another method to harness the power of Golden Love is via acts of service and compassion. By giving to others without expecting anything in return, we may tap into the power of unconditional love and begin to view the world through a new lens. This may bring a feeling of thankfulness and contentment that is not reliant on external conditions.

In conclusion, the power of Golden Love is a force that is accessible to us all. It is the sort of love that can alter our lives and the lives of others around us. By tapping into this power, we may achieve a feeling of inner peace and pleasure that is not reliant on external circumstances, and we can build a more loving and caring environment for everybody.

CHAPTER THREE

What is Eternal Bond?

The word "eternal bond" denotes a link or relationship that lasts endlessly, beyond the limitations of time and space. It talks of a profound, unbreakable connection between two or more humans, which continues eternally, surpassing the bounds of the physical world. The notion of an everlasting tie may be found in numerous cultures and faiths across the globe, and it bears a vital value in the lives of people.

At its root, an everlasting link is about a feeling of togetherness that transcends beyond the superficial or transitory. It is a relationship that is not founded on external events or situations, but rather on something deeper, more basic, and permanent. An everlasting tie may exist between friends, family members, or even between persons who have never met but have a shared bond, such as members of a spiritual community.

In many cultures, the notion of an everlasting link is related to the concept of soulmates. This theory argues that each individual has a unique, preset mate, someone with whom they are meant to spend forever. The relationship between soulmates is thought to be so strong that it can endure the rigors of time and distance, and even death itself.

But, an everlasting tie is not confined to romantic partnerships or soulmates. Intimacy may also exist between intimate friends, family members, or even between a person and a higher power or spiritual entity. For example, in Hinduism, the notion of "Rasaleela" alludes to the everlasting tie between

Krishna and his disciples. In this framework, the relationship between the person and the divine is considered indestructible, and it persists even after death.

One of the major elements of an everlasting relationship is that it is typically founded on shared experiences, values, or beliefs. This connection may be deepened by a feeling of mutual purpose or a shared vision for the future. When people develop a strong and meaningful link, they are more inclined to work together towards mutual objectives and support one another during tough times. In this manner, an immortal relationship may be a great force for good change in the world.

Nonetheless, it is vital to emphasize that an everlasting tie is not necessarily favorable or useful. In other situations, people may be bonded together by terrible events, such as trauma or abuse. These ties may be damaging and may need expert treatment to break away from. It is crucial to discern between good and harmful ties and to seek help when required.

In conclusion, the notion of an immortal tie reflects a profound and permanent relationship between persons that transcends time, space, and even death. It is a tremendous force for good change in the world, and it can bring people together in meaningful ways. Nonetheless, it is crucial to acknowledge that not all ties are healthy or useful and to seek assistance when required. Ultimately, an everlasting tie is a reflection of the inherent human yearning for connection and belonging, and it reminds us of the significance of creating meaningful connections in our lives.

The Importance of Everlasting Bond

The notion of an everlasting relationship has enormous importance in many cultures and communities across the globe. An everlasting link is a relationship between two persons that lasts beyond time, distance, and circumstance. It is a profound relationship that transcends the physical world and survives for eternity. In this article, we will analyze the value of an everlasting link and why it holds such importance to humans.

One of the most frequent instances of an everlasting link is the bond between two individuals in a love relationship. When two individuals fall in love, they frequently sense a profound connection that they think will endure forever. This relationship is sometimes referred to as an everlasting link, and it shows the depth of their love and dedication to each other. The importance of this lifelong link is that it brings a feeling of security and comfort to the pair. Knowing that they have each other for eternity adds a feeling of calm and security to their relationship. This permanent link also acts as a reminder to the couple to appreciate their relationship and to strive hard to sustain it.

Another example of an everlasting tie is the bond between a parent and a kid. When a kid is born, the parent-child link is created, and it is supposed to continue for eternity. This link is crucial because it reflects the unconditional love and support that a parent feels for their kid. The link between a parent and kid is one of the strongest ties that exist, and it can never be severed. This link gives the kid a feeling of security and comfort, knowing that they have a parent who will always be there for them, no matter what.

In certain traditions, an everlasting link is developed via a spiritual connection. For example, in Hinduism, it is believed that when two individuals are married, they develop a link that lasts for seven lives. This everlasting link signifies the notion of reincarnation and the belief that the two persons will be reunited in each lifetime. The importance of this everlasting link is that it promotes a sense of commitment and loyalty to the marriage. It is a reminder to the couple that they have pledged to each other that endures beyond this lifetime.

In many cultures, an everlasting relationship is also developed via friendship. When two individuals become friends, they frequently build a relationship that lasts for a lifetime. This relationship depicts the sense of loyalty, trust, and support that occurs between friends. The importance of this lifelong tie is that it brings a feeling of comfort and camaraderie to both persons. Knowing that they have a friend who will always be there for them, no matter what adds a feeling of pleasure and happiness to their life.

The value of an everlasting tie is also obvious in our interactions with animals. Many individuals create a close attachment with their dogs that lasts for a lifetime. This link depicts the notion of unconditional affection and devotion that occurs between an animal and its owner. The importance of this lifelong relationship is that it offers a feeling of comfort and friendship to the owner. Knowing that they have a pet that will always be there for them, no matter what adds a feeling of pleasure and contentment to their life.

In conclusion, the significance of an eternal bond is immense. It represents the idea of commitment, dedication, loyalty, trust, and support that exists between two individuals. Whether it be a sexual relationship, a parent-child link, a spiritual connection, a friendship, or a bond with an animal, an everlasting bond brings a feeling of security, comfort, and companionship to both persons. Knowing that they have someone or something that will always be there for them, no matter what adds a feeling of pleasure and contentment to their life. The notion of an everlasting tie is a strong one, and it reminds us of the significance of our relationships with people and the value of these interactions in our lives.

Creating Everlasting Connection.

Establishing an everlasting tie is a notion that incorporates many elements of human relationships, including friendships, romantic engagements, and familial bonds. At its essence, it refers to the forging of a relationship that is powerful, durable, and significant, with a feeling of devotion and dedication that transcends well beyond the present. In this article, I will analyze the numerous components of forming an everlasting link and why it is crucial for human development.

At the core of every enduring tie is trust. Trust is the basis upon which all good relationships are founded. When we trust someone, we feel comfortable with them, and we can depend on them to be there for us when we need them. Trust is created over time via consistent conduct and honest communication. When we feel that we can trust someone, we are more inclined to open up to them and reveal our innermost thoughts and emotions, which may lead to deeper relationships.

Another crucial component of forming an enduring friendship is respect. When we respect someone, we appreciate them for who they are, regardless of their faults or limitations. Respect implies treating people as we would want to be treated ourselves, with love, compassion, and understanding. When we respect someone, we are more inclined to listen to them and take their thoughts and emotions into consideration, which may lead to more empathy and understanding.

Communication is also vital for developing an enduring friendship. When we speak freely and honestly with others, we establish an atmosphere of trust and respect. Communication helps us to communicate our thoughts and emotions, express our needs and aspirations, and work through disputes and obstacles together. When we communicate successfully, we are more likely to feel heard and understood, which may lead to a greater relationship with others.

Another key part of developing an enduring link is shared experiences. As we share experiences with people, we build memories that we can look back on jointly, enhancing our relationship. Shared experiences may be simple, like going for a stroll or having a meal, or they can be more substantial, like traveling to a new area or conquering a struggle together. Regardless of the nature of the encounter, it is the common relationship that establishes the enduring connection.

Ultimately, developing an everlasting link demands a feeling of commitment and devotion. When we are dedicated to someone, we are willing to put time, energy, and effort into the connection, even when it is tough. Commitment involves being there for someone when they need us, even when it is unpleasant or uncomfortable. When we are devoted and dedicated to someone, we build a feeling of devotion that can last even in the worst of situations.

To conclude, developing an everlasting relationship is a difficult process that includes a mix of trust, respect, communication, shared experiences, and dedication. When we engage in these components of a relationship, we develop relationships that are deep, persistent, and meaningful. These ties may provide us with a feeling of pleasure, contentment, and purpose, and can be vital for our general well-being. Hence, whether it is with a friend, a partner, or a family member, let us endeavor to develop everlasting relationships that will survive the test of time.

Pure Affection

Pure affection refers to an emotional condition of love and compassion that is free from any selfish or materialistic reasons. It is a real emotion of love and care that arises from the heart and is given to someone without any expectations of gaining something in return. Pure love is defined by its selflessness, unconditional nature, and its capacity to transcend any borders or constraints.

Pure affection may be found in different sorts of relationships, including romantic love, parental love, platonic love, and even love for one's pet or a beloved activity. In all these interactions, pure love is distinguished by the lack of any ulterior goals or hidden objectives. It is a sentiment that is expressed completely out of a desire to love and care for another person or object.

In romantic partnerships, pure affection is generally characterized as a sense of love that is not reliant on physical attractiveness or monetary rewards. It is a sensation that comes from a profound emotional connection between two people, and it is not based on external variables such as income, prestige, or physical attractiveness. Pure love in romantic relationships is defined by its capacity to survive the test of time and conquer any difficulties or problems that may occur.

In parental love, pure affection is typically considered as the unconditional love that a parent feels for their kid. It is a love that is not dependent on the child's accomplishments or conduct but on the basic fact of their being. Pure affection in parental love is characterized by its ability to forgive, nurture, and provide a sense of security and stability to the child.

In platonic love, pure affection is often described as a feeling of love and care that is not based on any romantic or sexual attraction. It is a love that arises from a deep connection between two people, based on shared interests, values, and experiences. Pure affection in platonic love is characterized by its ability to provide a sense of companionship, support, and understanding, without any expectations of getting anything in return.

Pure affection may also be seen in the love that individuals feel for their pets, or a specific pastime or passion. In these instances, pure attachment is defined by the delight and happiness that comes from being with the object of one's affection. It is a love that is not based on any monetary rewards but on the simple pleasure of being able to spend one's time and energy with something that offers joy and fullness to one's life.

In conclusion, pure affection is a sense of love and caring that is free from any selfish or materialistic objectives. It is a sincere expression of love that originates from the heart and is directed towards someone or something without any expectations of gaining anything in return. Pure affection may be found in different sorts of relationships, including romantic love, parental love, platonic love, and even love for one's pet or a beloved activity. It is a feeling that is characterized by its selflessness, unconditional nature, and its ability to transcend any boundaries or limitations. Pure love is a strong force that may bring pleasure, happiness, and satisfaction to people's lives, and it is something that should be treasured and appreciated.

Features of Pure Love

Pure affection is a word that refers to the deepest level of love that one may have for another human. This sort of love is defined by a distinct collection of traits that separate it from other forms of love. In this post, we will investigate 10 aspects of pure affection, explaining what each one implies and how it contributes to this sort of love.

1. Unconditional: One of the fundamental qualities of pure love is that it is unconditional. This signifies that love is not reliant on any circumstances, such as the other person's conduct or acts. Instead, it is offered freely and without expectation of anything in return.

2. Selfless: True love is likewise selfless. This indicates that the attention is on the other person and their needs, rather than on oneself. The individual feeling pure love is prepared to sacrifice their wishes and needs for the benefit of the other person.

3. Genuine: Pure affection is defined by real sentiments of love and affection for the other person.

There is no pretense or insincerity in this form of love. It is built on a sincere appreciation for the other person and their attributes.

4. Empathetic: Pure attachment implies a great degree of empathy. This implies that the one experiencing this form of love can comprehend and share the other person's thoughts and experiences. They can imagine themselves in the other person's situation and react with compassion and caring.

5. Respectful: Another quality of pure attachment is that it is respectful. This indicates that the individual experiencing this form of love respects the other person with decency and honor. They appreciate the other person's thoughts, emotions, and needs, and they do not ridicule or ignore them.

6. Forgiving: Absolute love implies a great degree of forgiveness. This implies that the person

experiencing this form of love can ignore the other person's defects and shortcomings and react with compassion and understanding. They are prepared to forgive and move on, rather than clinging to grudges or hatred.

7. Patient: True love also demands a great lot of patience. This signifies that the individual experiencing this form of love is willing to wait for the other person to develop and evolve. They recognize that personal progress takes time and they are eager to help and encourage the other person along the road.

8. Trusting: Pure attachment is characterized by a great degree of trust. This signifies that the individual experiencing this form of love trusts the other person entirely. They trust in the other person's decency and honesty, and they do not feel the need to continually watch or manage them.

9. Joyful: Absolute affection is a wonderful feeling. This indicates that the individual experiencing this form of love gets a great feeling of satisfaction and fulfillment while they are with the other person. They like spending time together and they find contentment in their relationship.

10. Lasting: Eventually, genuine love is enduring. This signifies that love is not ephemeral or temporary, but rather it sustains throughout time. The individual experiencing this form of love is devoted to the other person for the long haul, and they are ready to weather any storms that come their way.

Additionally, pure affection may have a transforming influence on both the individual feeling the love and the person receiving it. When we are the receiver of genuine love, we feel seen, heard, and cherished. This may lead to greater self-esteem and a feeling of belonging. On the other side, when we feel genuine adoration for another person, we become more empathetic, patient, and understanding. We learn to recognize the positive characteristics of people and to look past their imperfections.

Genuine love may also have a favorable influence on our physical and mental well-being. Research has indicated that persons who feel love and affection are less likely to have depression, anxiety, and other mental health concerns. They are also more likely to have stronger immune systems and higher physical fitness.

Although pure affection is commonly linked with romantic love, it may be experienced in any form of connection, including friendships, familial ties, and even with pets. The crucial thing is that the love be sincere and unconditional.

But, true love is not always simple to come by. It involves a tremendous level of self-awareness, vulnerability, and emotional maturity. It may also be tough to sustain pure love over time, particularly when confronted with disagreements and problems in the partnership.

To create pure love in our relationships, we might start by exercising empathy, forgiveness, and respect. We may also concentrate on increasing our emotional intelligence and communication abilities. By learning to communicate our own needs and emotions healthily, we can provide a safe and supportive environment for others to do the same.

In addition, it's crucial to prioritize the connection and make time for the other person. This might entail spending quality time together, participating in activities that are significant to both people, and being present and attentive while together. It's also crucial to express respect and thanks for the other person and to appreciate their victories and accomplishments.

In conclusion, pure affection is a strong type of love that can alter our relationships and our lives. Although it may be tough to acquire, it is worth working for in every relationship. By exercising empathy, forgiveness, and respect, and by prioritizing the connection, we may create a place for pure attachment to bloom. When we feel pure love, we have a great sense of pleasure and delight, and we can form strong and enduring relationships with people.

Importance of Pure Compassion

1. Provides a feeling of belonging: Pure love generates a sense of belonging and connection with others. When we feel liked and respected, we are more likely to have a feeling of belonging in our families, communities, and social organizations. This feeling of belonging may help us feel safe and confident in our relationships, which can have a good influence on our mental health and well-being.

2. Builds trust: True love is founded on trust and honesty. When we have a genuine love for someone, we trust them and are open and honest with them. This gives a feeling of safety and security in our interactions, which may help us form better ties with others.

3. Increases communication: Pure love may promote effective communication in relationships. When we

feel appreciated and cherished, we are more willing to communicate our ideas and emotions honestly and freely. This may help us interact better with others and develop deeper, more meaningful relationships.

4. Increases empathy: Absolute love creates empathy and compassion toward others. When we feel liked and respected, we are more inclined to be empathetic toward others and comprehend their viewpoints. This may help us form greater ties with people and create a more peaceful society.

5. Enhances well-being: Pure love may increase our bodily and mental well-being. When we feel liked and respected, we are more likely to experience pleasant feelings such as pleasure, happiness, and satisfaction. This may have a good influence on our mental health and well-being and can help deal with stress and hardship.

6. Fosters personal growth: Absolute love may stimulate personal growth and development. When we feel loved and valued, we are more inclined to feel confident in ourselves and our talents. This may help us pursue our goals and dreams and become the greatest version of ourselves.

7. Strengthens family relationships: Genuine love is crucial for building family bonds. When family members feel respected, they are more likely to support and care for one another. This may build a strong feeling of family togetherness and can help families endure obstacles and hardship together.

8. Supports social peace: Pure attachment may foster social harmony and lessen conflict in the society. When individuals feel loved and cherished, they are more inclined to be tolerant and welcoming of

others. This may help establish a more inclusive and peaceful society.

9. Creates a good legacy: Pure love may generate a positive legacy that lasts for generations. When we express true compassion toward others, we develop a culture of love and kindness that may be handed down from generation to generation. This may help build a more compassionate and caring environment for future generations.

Genuine love is very crucial for forging strong, meaningful relationships and producing a more peaceful society. It develops empathy, trust, and honesty, and it boosts our well-being and personal progress. By nurturing genuine love for others, we may build a more positive and loving environment for ourselves and future generations.

CHAPTER FOUR

The Voyage of Golden Love

Beginning the path of Golden Love may be a transforming experience that leads to a stronger feeling of connection and satisfaction in your love relationship. Golden Love is defined by a profound and unconditional love that is built on a mutual understanding and respect for each other's needs, wants, and desires.

If you're ready to go on the path of Golden Love, here are some recommendations to get you started:

1. Develop self-love and self-acceptance: Before you can fully love another person, you must first love and accept yourself. This includes learning to

accept your talents and shortcomings, appreciating your oddities and defects, and treating yourself with respect and compassion. Take time to explore your passions, hobbies, and interests and emphasize self-care techniques that feed your mind, body, and spirit.

2. Define your values and priorities: Understanding what you value and prioritize in life is vital for finding a spouse who shares your objectives and ambitions. Take some time to think about what means most to you, whether it's family, job, faith, or personal improvement. After you've established your essential beliefs, utilize them as a guide while considering possible partners and managing your relationships.

3. Practice open and honest communication: Good communication is vital for developing healthy and rewarding relationships. Be willing to share your

opinions and emotions freely and honestly, while also listening to and respecting your partner's viewpoint. Avoid making assumptions or leaping to conclusions and accept responsibility for your own emotions and behaviors.

4. Nurture trust and intimacy: Trust and intimacy are the pillars of Golden Love. Build trust by being consistent and dependable, honoring your commitments, and being honest and straightforward. Intimacy may be developed via physical contact, emotional vulnerability, and shared experiences. Take time to connect with your spouse on a deep level and establish a secure and supportive atmosphere where you can be yourself and express your love freely.

5. Accept vulnerability and forgiveness: No relationship is flawless, and there will be moments when you or your spouse make errors or hurt one

other's emotions. Accept vulnerability by being ready to recognize your faults and apologize when required. Exercise forgiveness by letting go of grudges and resentments and choosing to move ahead with love and compassion.

6. Make time for romance and fun: Although creating a solid foundation of trust, communication, and intimacy is crucial, it's equally necessary to make time for romance and fun in your relationship. Arrange date evenings, surprise your spouse with meaningful gestures, and participate in activities that offer you both delight and excitement.

7. Constantly develop and learn together: The path of Golden Love is a lifetime process of growth and learning. Accept the ups and downs of your relationship as a chance for personal and relational development. Study books or attend seminars on relationships, talk clearly about your wants and

aspirations and be prepared to try new things and take chances together.

Beginning the path of Golden Love involves patience, self-awareness, and a desire to be vulnerable and real. By cultivating self-love, clarifying your values, practicing open communication, fostering trust and intimacy, embracing vulnerability and forgiveness, making time for romance and fun, and continuously growing and learning together, you can create a relationship that is grounded in love, mutual respect, and deep connection.

Difficulties Along the Road.

Love is a lovely journey that many individuals go upon, expecting to attain the ultimate happiness of a satisfying and long-lasting relationship. Yet, the journey to "golden love" is not always straightforward, and there are problems that every couple must encounter along the way. In the subsequent pages, we will cover 13 problems that lovers typically confront along the road of Golden Love.

1. Communication: Communication is a cornerstone of every successful relationship. But, communication may be tough when couples come from different backgrounds or have distinct communication styles. Couples must learn to successfully express their emotions and wants, without harming one another in the process.

2. Trust: Trust is crucial to a good relationship, but it is not always simple to create. The trust may be eroded through adultery, deceit, or even simple behaviors that weaken the link between two

individuals. Restoring trust requires time and effort, and sometimes it is not feasible to rebuild the trust that was lost.

3. Compatibility: Compatibility refers to how well two individuals fit together in terms of personality, interests, and values. Although opposites may attract, they may also lead to problems and misunderstandings. Couples must learn to respect one another's peculiarities and establish common ground.

4. Intimacy: Intimacy is an essential feature of a love relationship. But, it may be tough when one partner has a larger sex desire than the other, or when physical or mental hurdles stand in the way. Couples must develop methods to be intimate that work for both parties.

5. Finances: Money may be a cause of stress and tension in every relationship. Disagreements about spending habits, debt, or wealth inequalities may undermine a couple's connection. Couples must learn to handle their money jointly, and make choices that benefit both spouses.

6. Time Management: Tight schedules and competing priorities may make it tough for couples to find time for each other. Balancing job, family, and social duties may lead to emotions of neglect or anger. Couples must prioritize their relationship and make time for each other.

7. Family and Friends: Family and friends may be a source of support and affection, but they can also generate tension in a romantic relationship. In-laws, ex-partners, and interfering friends might interfere with a couple's relationship. Couples must learn to create boundaries and convey their needs to others.

8. Jealousy: Jealousy may be a damaging factor in a relationship, leading to insecurity, distrust, and even dominating behavior. Jealousy might come from prior traumas, anxieties, or sentiments of possessiveness. Couples must learn to address the core reasons for envy and develop strategies to establish trust.

9. Personal Growth: Personal development is a vital component of every individual's life, but it may also produce friction in a relationship. As one spouse matures and changes, the other may feel left behind or threatened. Couples must learn to encourage one another's progress and discover methods to grow together.

10. Conflict Resolution: Conflict is inherent in every relationship. How couples manage disagreement may build or destroy their connection. Couples must

learn to settle problems healthily and productively, without turning to blame, judgment, or cruel remarks.

11. Prioritizing the Relationship: In a busy and demanding environment, it may be tough to prioritize a love connection. Career, hobbies, and personal objectives might take priority over a partner's needs. Couples must learn to put their relationship first and make sacrifices for one another.

12. Distance: Distance may offer a big difficulty for couples, whether it is physical or emotional. Long-distance relationships, work-related travel, or emotional distance may weaken a couple's connection. Couples must discover methods to remain connected and sustain their closeness, even while they are away.

14. Aging: Aging is a normal part of life, and it may bring both physical and emotional changes that might damage a relationship. As people age, their objectives, hobbies, and physical capacities may vary. Couples must learn to adapt to these changes and discover methods to develop and flourish together.

Although these problems may appear formidable, they are not insurmountable. Conquering these problems may enhance a couple's connection and lead to a deeper and more rewarding relationship. Here are some tips for navigating these challenges:

1. Communication: Employ active listening and empathy, and be honest and straightforward in your communication.
2Trust: Be honest and consistent in your behaviors, and make attempts to reestablish trust if it has been eroded.

3. Compatibility: Concentrate on finding common ground and embrace each other's uniqueness.

4. Intimacy: Be open and honest about your wants and desires, and create methods to connect that work for both parties.

5. Finances: Establish financial objectives together and talk freely about spending habits and priorities.

6. Time Management: Make quality time a priority and discover methods to arrange it into your hectic life.

7. Family and Friends: Establish boundaries and explain your requirements to others, while still being respectful of their relationships with your spouse.

8. Jealousy: Address the fundamental reasons for jealousy and focus on creating trust via open communication and openness.

9. Personal Growth: Encourage each other's development and create methods to grow together, while simultaneously keeping your uniqueness.

10. Conflict Resolution: Employ active listening and compromise, and avoid blaming or assaulting one another during arguments.

11. Prioritizing the Relationship: Make sacrifices for each other and place your connection above other duties.

12. Distance: Discover strategies to remain connected, such as frequent contact or scheduled visits.

13. Aging: Accept the changes that occur with age and discover methods to adapt and progress together.

In conclusion, the road to Golden Love is not without its problems, but these challenges may be conquered with work and determination. By practicing good communication, creating trust, finding common ground, and prioritizing your relationship, you can manage these hurdles and create a strong and enduring connection with your spouse. Remember, every relationship is unique, and what works for one couple may not work for another. Discover what works for you and your spouse and enjoy the adventure of love together.

The Final Destination of Golden Love.

Golden love is a word used to describe a lasting and genuinely rewarding relationship that survives the test of time. It is a love that is unselfish, unconditional, and pure. Although many individuals want to attain this sort of love, few realize the ultimate goal of golden love.

The ultimate goal of golden love is not a geographical location, but a state of being. It is a feeling of total happiness and fulfillment that can only be obtained by a profound relationship with another person. Golden love is not about finding someone who can complete us, but about finding someone who can complement us and bring out the best in us.

The path toward golden love may be long and arduous, but the benefits are tremendous. It involves patience, effort, and a willingness to be vulnerable. It entails placing the needs of the other person above our own and making sacrifices for their satisfaction. That means embracing and loving them for who they are, warts and all.

The ultimate objective of golden love is a condition of perfect acceptance and understanding. It is a condition in which we feel entirely known and completely cherished. It is a condition in which we may be ourselves without fear of criticism or rejection. In this condition, we feel comfortable, protected, and supported.

Golden love is not about perfection, but about progress. It is about developing together as individuals and as a partnership. It is about learning from one another's talents and flaws and utilizing that information to become better individuals. It is about tackling hardships together and coming out stronger on the other side.

The ultimate objective of golden love is not simply a state of being, but a method of life. It is about living with purpose and meaning and having a good effect on the world around us. It is about utilizing our love as a force for good, and spreading pleasure and happiness everywhere we go.

In conclusion, the ultimate objective of golden love is a state of perfect joy, fulfillment, and pleasure. It is a state that can only be created by a profound relationship with another person and needs patience, dedication, and vulnerability. Although the path toward golden love might be lengthy and arduous, the benefits are incomparable. It is a condition of being that brings out the best in us and helps us to live with purpose and meaning.

Personal Effects of Golden Love

Golden Love may have a powerful influence on people, as it can touch the deepest elements of their being and alter them in ways that they may never have imagined possible.

At its essence, Golden Love is distinguished by its selflessness. It is the sort of love that is ready to make sacrifices for the well-being of the other person. This form of love is not conditional or reliant on what the other person can supply, but rather on a profound feeling of caring and commitment. When an individual experiences Golden Love, they may feel a sense of warmth and comfort that they may have never felt before. This can lead to feelings of security and confidence, as they know that they have someone who cares for them deeply.

Golden Love can also have a transformative impact on an individual's sense of self. When someone experiences this type of love, they may feel a sense of worthiness and belonging that they may have never felt before. This can lead to a greater sense of self-esteem and self-confidence, as they know that they are loved and valued for who they are. This can have a ripple effect on all areas of their life, as they may feel more empowered to pursue their goals and dreams.

Furthermore, Golden Love can also impact an individual's relationships with others. When someone experiences this type of love, they may feel more inclined to show compassion and kindness to others. This can lead to stronger and more meaningful connections with friends, family, and even strangers. Golden Love can also help individuals to let go of grudges and resentments, as they realize that the only way to truly love someone is to forgive them for their faults and shortcomings.

Finally, Golden Love can also impact an individual's sense of purpose and meaning in life. When someone experiences this type of love, they may feel a greater sense of connection to the world around them. This can lead to a desire to make a positive impact on the world and to contribute to something larger than themselves. They may also feel a greater sense of gratitude for the blessings in their life, which can lead to a more positive outlook on life.

In conclusion, Golden Love may have a tremendous influence on humans in many different ways. It may touch the deepest portions of their being and alter them in ways that they may never have dreamed possible. It may affect their sense of self, their connections with others, and their sense of purpose and meaning in life. Finally, Golden Love is a reminder that love is the most powerful force in the world, and that it can heal, change, and inspire us all.

Social Effects of Golden Love.

Golden Love is a word that represents a sort of love that is pure, unselfish, and unconditional. It is the sort of love that individuals desire to have in their relationships, and it has a huge influence on society. The concept of Golden Love has been around for centuries, but its societal impact has become more apparent in recent times.

One of the most significant impacts of Golden Love on society is its ability to foster deeper connections between individuals. When people approach relationships with a Golden Love mentality, they prioritize the needs of their loved ones over their own. This leads to a stronger sense of empathy and understanding, which can lead to better communication and more fulfilling relationships. When individuals are connected in this way, they are more likely to work together towards common goals, leading to a more harmonious society.

Golden Love also has a favorable influence on mental wellness. When individuals feel loved and supported, they are more likely to experience positive emotions such as happiness, contentment, and fulfillment. This can lead to increased confidence and self-esteem, which in turn can improve overall mental health. Research has indicated that persons in meaningful relationships are less likely to suffer from depression, anxiety, and other mental health concerns.

Additionally, the notion of Golden Love has a favorable influence on the family unit. When parents love their children unconditionally, it provides a secure and loving atmosphere where children may grow and develop. Children who grow up in loving households are more likely to have a good self-image, greater social skills, and higher levels of academic accomplishment. When families emphasize Golden Love, it generates a ripple effect that may favorably benefit the whole community.

Golden Love may also have a huge influence on social justice concerns. When individuals approach relationships with a Golden Love perspective, they are more likely to be sensitive and understanding towards others who are different from them. This may lead to more tolerance and acceptance of individuals from diverse origins, beliefs, and cultures. It may also lead to a higher readiness to fight against social injustices such as racism, sexism, and homophobia.

In conclusion, Golden Love is a strong force that has a good influence on society in many ways. It develops stronger relationships between people, enhances mental health, strengthens the family unit, and promotes social justice. As individuals, when we approach our relationships with a Golden Love perspective, we create a better world for ourselves and those around us. When we prioritize the needs of others before our own, we build a culture that is more compassionate, empathic, and welcoming.

Romantic Love Story.

Two persons encountered each other under the most unexpected circumstances. They both were working at a little coffee shop in the center of the city. Sandy was a barista who liked to work with coffee, and she was constantly smiling at people that visited the café. Enoch was a frequent client who used to come to the café every morning to collect his cup of coffee before work. He was usually on time, and Sandy could see him from a distance.

One day, when Enoch was standing in line to purchase his coffee, Sandy unintentionally spilled coffee on him. She was so humiliated that she apologized a million times and offered to buy him a new shirt. Enoch laughed it off, and they began conversing. They chatted about their favorite coffee blends, their favorite movies, and their favorite locations to visit. They both felt a closeness that they had never felt before.

Sandy and Enoch began to see one other more regularly following that day. Enoch would come to the café even on his days off, and they would sit and speak for hours. They both felt that there was something special between them, but they were too terrified to acknowledge it to one other. They both had been injured in the past, and they didn't want to hurry into anything.

Months passed by, and Sandy and Enoch became closer and closer. They had a profound knowledge of each other, and they recognized each other's talents and flaws. They had created a kinship that they couldn't ignore any longer. They both realized that they were in love with one other.

Yet just when everything was going well, life threw them a curveball. Sandy's mother was unwell and had to be hospitalized. Sandy was upset, and she didn't know what to do. Enoch was there for her every step of the way. He supported her, hugged her when she sobbed and made sure that she realized that she wasn't alone. Sandy felt that she had discovered someone unique, someone, who loved her for who she was.

Once her mother died, Sandy learned that life was too short to spend time on things that didn't matter. She realized that she wanted to spend the rest of her life with Enoch. But before she could inform him, Enoch received a job offer in another state. He didn't know what to do. He loved Sandy, but he also liked his work. He didn't want to leave her behind, but he also didn't want to give up his ambition.

Sandy was devastated. She didn't want to lose Enoch, but she didn't want to hold him back either. They both understood that their love was powerful, but they also realized that it was going to be tough. They spoke about it, and they agreed that they were going to give their relationship a try. Enoch accepted the position, but he pledged to see Sandy any time he had. They both understood that it was going to be hard, but they were eager to try.

The following several months were trying for Sandy and Enoch. They had to depend on phone conversations and video chats to keep in contact. They missed each other badly, but they were determined to make it work. Enoch would give Sandy flowers and presents to show her how much he loved her. Sandy would send him care packages to remind him of home. They both understood that they had something unique, and they weren't going to let distance get in the way.

Yet just when they believed that things were beginning to look up, another roadblock came their way. Sandy's father suffered a heart attack and required a bypass operation. Sandy was upset, and she didn't know what to do. Enoch understood that he had to be there for her, no matter what. He took a leave of absence from work and traveled back to be with Sandy. He remained with her in the hospital for days, holding her hand and making sure that she understood that she wasn't alone.

Sandy was thankful for Enoch's encouragement, and she felt that he was the one for her. She couldn't picture her life without him. They both realized that they wanted to spend the rest of their lives together.

Following her father's successful operation, Enoch and Sandy chatted about their future. They understood that they had gone through a lot, but they also knew that they had a deep tie that could survive anything. They made the decision to become engaged as the next step.

Enoch proposed to Sandy on the rooftop in the city. He had planned the entire affair, and he had even arranged for a photographer to record the occasion. Sandy was filled with emotion, and she replied yes without hesitation. They both realized that they had a lot of work ahead of them, but they were ready to tackle together. Arranging a wedding was hectic, but Sandy and Enoch knew that they wanted to make it memorable. They wanted to honor their love and their journey together. They wanted to share their excitement with their family and friends. The day of the wedding approached, and Sandy was apprehensive. She wanted everything to be perfect, but she also realized that the most essential thing was to marry Enoch. When she proceeded down the aisle, she found Enoch waiting for her with tears in his eyes. They exchanged vows, and they both knew that they had met their soulmate.

Their marriage wasn't always easy, but they both understood that they were destined to be together. They supported each other through tough times, and they shared each other's accomplishments. They knew that their love was strong enough to weather anything that life threw their way. Years passed by, and Enoch and Sandy established a life together. They had children, and they saw them grow up into beautiful, accomplished individuals. They had their ups and downs, but they always remained committed to each other. They both understood that they had discovered something wonderful, something that many people never get to experience. While they sat on their front porch, watching the sunset, Sandy glanced at Enoch and remarked, "I never believed that I could love someone as much as I love you." Enoch grinned and added, "I feel the same way. You are my everything." Enoch and

Sandy began their passionate relationship in a coffee shop, experienced numerous hardships, and finally married happily.

They demonstrated that genuine love can transcend anything and that sometimes the best love tales emerge from unexpected beginnings.

As they got older, they never lost the spark in their love. They continued to go on date nights, take vacations together, and find time for one another despite their hectic lives. They realized that their love was something exceptional, and they never took it for granted.

As they celebrated their 50th wedding anniversary, their children and grandkids gave them a tremendous celebration. When they glanced around at the room packed with their loved ones, Sandy couldn't help but feel happy for the life that they had established together.

At the party, their granddaughter asked them, "What's the key to a long and happy marriage?" They glanced at each other and grinned.

"We've always placed one other first," Sandy added. "We've been there for each other through thick and thin, and we've never let our love slip away."

Enoch said, "And we constantly communicate. We speak about anything, even when it's painful." Their children and grandkids listened closely, taking in their wisdom. They understood that they had been lucky to experience a love like Enoch and Sandy's

As the party wound down, Enoch and Sandy sat in their living room holding hands. They looked back on their journey together and we're pleased with everything that they had achieved. They had constructed a life filled with love, pleasure, and memories that they would treasure forever. As they got ready for bed, Enoch turned to Sandy and remarked, "I still can't believe that we began our passionate love in a coffee shop all those years ago."

Sandy smiled and answered, "That just goes to show that sometimes the most beautiful love tales may start in the most unexpected locations." Enoch and Sandy's love story is a tribute to the power of real and golden love. They began as strangers at a coffee shop and endured numerous hurdles, yet their love stayed strong. They demonstrated that genuine love is not only about joyful moments, but it's also about supporting one other through terrible times.

Their marriage was not flawless, but it was full of love, understanding, and respect. They proved that communication and putting each other first were the key to a happy marriage. They were each other's support through all that life threw their way.

In the end, Enoch and Sandy's love story is a reminder that genuine love is attainable, and it's worth fighting for. Their love tale will continue to inspire others for centuries to come.

CONCLUSION

Golden love is a wonderful thing, a unique and beautiful gift that provides pleasure and happiness to our life. Whether we are young or old, affluent or poor, love has the potential to alter us, to make us better, stronger, and more satisfied. In conclusion, I would like to share with you some ideas about golden love, its significance, and how it enhances our lives.

Golden love is not only an emotion but a commitment, a choice to remain with someone through thick and thin, to support them, to encourage them, and to share their joys and sorrows. It is a relationship founded on trust, respect, and mutual understanding, a tie that becomes stronger with time.

Golden love is also about forgiving, letting go of past wounds, and enjoying the current moment. It is about embracing one another's faults and defects and loving each other despite them. It is about being patient, kind, and empathetic, and constantly placing the needs of our partner before our own.

Golden love is a source of inspiration, a fountain of creativity, and a wellspring of happiness. It fills our hearts with delight, our brains with wonder, and our souls with tranquility. It encourages us to be our best selves, to strive for greatness, and to live our lives with purpose and meaning.

Therefore if you are fortunate enough to have discovered golden love, cherish it, cultivate it, and guard it with all your heart. Because it is a treasure beyond measure, a gift from the heavens, a blessing that will improve your life and the lives of others around you. And if you have yet to discover it, do not despair, because love is always within reach, waiting for you to open your heart and accept its enchantment.

In conclusion, golden love is a wonderful thing, a priceless gift that enhances our lives in various ways. It is a commitment, a relationship, and a source of inspiration that fills our hearts with pleasure and our souls with tranquility. So let us all appreciate love, embrace it, and enjoy its beauty and wonder, because it is indeed the greatest gift of all.

www.ingramcontent.com/pod-product-compliance
Lightning Source LLC
Chambersburg PA
CBHW070558220526
45467CB00003B/1239